Moving Forward:

You, Like Me, Can Overcome

By Diana Clarke, Ph.D.

Moving Forward: You, Like, Me Can Overcome

ISBN 978-1-79685-593-7 (paperback)

Foreword

Moving Forward: You, Like Me, Can Overcome, is an amazing book that provides strength and motivation where conflict and hardship exist. This book will provide inspiration to those who have experienced the type of difficult, traumatic, and life changing challenges that often immobilize and disable. The stories and lessons shared with the book show how persistence, perseverance, and determination can overcome all obstacles. Despite the severity and complexities of her circumstances, the author has provided the details of how she was able to follow her dreams, stay focused on her goals, and move forward to create a successful and positive life. The author's life story empowers, provides insight, and sets the example for women around the world who face obstacles and barriers that appear to be designed to stop and derail their efforts to achieve the life they deserve.

Moving Forward: You, Like Me, Can Overcome is an excellent source of power and strength for women of all ages.

Dr. Alfred. S. Titus, Jr.
A. Titus Consulting, LLC.

Foreword

From an academic viewpoint, Dr. Clarke's book is timely and useful. The book is a true testimony of overcoming sexual abuse and assault, learning to trust and love again, and finding a sense of self-worth. It is a testimony because sexual abuse often occurs at an early age and remain dormant well into adulthood. When left untreated, lifetime results are visible in the form of PTSD, depression, and anxiety. The trauma of sexual assault or violence can affect the mind and body's ability to process what occurred, leading to different emotions, behaviors, and physical responses that rollercoaster between appearing, disappearing, and reappearing.

The book is timely because broken homes are more prevalent than ever. Single parenting has become commonplace, with the mother bearing the majority of the role and responsibilities typically held by the father. In many cases, being the only provider often requires taking on multiple jobs to meet financial demands that range from child care, rent/mortgage, transportation, food and clothing, etc. This ultimately may cause the child to spend countless hours with another family member, or with one or multiple friends of the single parent.

The book is useful because it provides indicators and effects of sexual abuse by a family member or another supposedly trustworthy adult. However, every child and situation may differ. Therefore, Dr. Clarke's experience is one of many females that may share one or more encounters of sexual abuse or assault. The book also details her own personal dealings with absent parents, sexual abuse by family members, uncertainty in relationships, teenage pregnancy, single parenting, educational demands, finding her sense of self, and becoming an advocate for other young females.

Dr. Clarke has dedicated her professional career to working with youth at-risk females who may have been, or may be, a victim of sexual abuse or assault. Having founded a nonprofit organization, Move Beyond, Inc., Dr. Clarke's vision is to influence young adults to use their strategic planning, resources, and self-resilience to move beyond past failures and doubts and toward success. The organization's mission is to strengthen our communities by empowering young people with knowledge and guidance to reach their full potential through mentorship, education, and positive relationships.

By hosting annual motivational summits, and being a key motivational speaker, Dr. Clarke and her board member's goal is to take Move Beyond, Inc. to the next level. Dr. Clarke has built her nonprofit organization on a spiritual foundation of faith in her works, and trusts that her works will direct her path to achieving longevity in her foundation. More importantly, increasing the awareness of sexual abuse or assault.

Finally, I would like to commend Dr. Clarke for her courage to share her testimony. This book is a beacon that not only illuminates the dark world of sexual abuse and assault, it is a symbol of inspiration, hope, and speaks volume to the power within a victim to reclaim their life.

by Dr. Lonnie Brinson
Adjunct Professor, American Public University
Adjunct Assistant Professor, Embry Riddle Aeronautical University

Preface

I wrote this book as a motivational tool for a specific audience: Individuals who have experienced, and are still experiencing, risk factors hindering them from achieving their goals. Individuals who have given up on trying to become a better person. Individuals who allow themselves to be conquered by circumstances beyond their control. Individuals who are allowing societal and research statistics to dictate their future. Individuals who continue to struggle with feelings of worthlessness and low self-esteem.

Last, but not least, I wrote this book to encourage individuals who have the desire to move beyond past hurts and pain, failures, and doubts, but put limitations on their capability to do so. It is my prayer and sincere desire that this book will empower you to start your journey.

Acknowledgements

Who would have thought I would write a book? Certainly not me. Even a year ago, I was still trying to avoid this journey.

What a difference it makes when you have great supporters who encourage you, pushing you out of your comfort zone to remove all the limitations.

First, I want to thank my mother, Mrs. Hilda Wright, for understanding my purpose in writing this book and supporting me in doing so. I admire the strong woman that you are. You are such a blessing in my life; I love and appreciate you dearly.

Second, to my sisters and brothers, words cannot explain how much I appreciate your support, encouragement, and understanding during this process. In addition, you taking time from your busy schedules to meet with me, listen, and discuss the content of this book strengthened my desire to write and publish it.

Third, to my late father, Hector Clarke: Even though I spent only a very short time with you, I will always treasure the one instruction you gave me: to achieve the highest level of education and be an independent woman.

Fourth, to the men who intentionally caused me pain, suffering, and anger, though your contribution to my life was negative, it shaped me to become the woman I am today. You are forgiven!

Last, but not least, my children, Tiffanie, Tevaris, and Tavious. You are my rock, my main motivators, my world. I have no words to explain how grateful I am to be your mother. You struggled with me and at times went without, yet you never complained. There were days when everything seemed dark and I wanted to quit, but you kept me going. I have always believed if God did not entrust me with you, I would probably have given up a long time ago. Thanks for your support along this journey. I love you, beautiful lady and handsome fellows!

It would be injustice if I closed without mentioning my maternal grandparents, the late Mr. and Mrs. Ritchie. Thank you for not only being my grandparents, but also my parents. You provided, you taught, you disciplined, you loved, you cared, you molded, you guided. You went above and beyond your roles.

I also need to acknowledge my cousin, Kenneth, who supported me wholeheartedly, even with his reservation about the book's impact on our family.

To my work family, Andrea, Shemina, Shayna, and Jeneen, thanks for encouraging me for pursing this journey and not allowing me to give up when times were hard.

To Dr. Alfred Titus, thank you for all your assistance.

Finally, thank you to Dr. Laura Schlater, who not only provided editorial services but bought this book to life. Your work is greatly appreciated.

Table of Contents

Introduction

On November 22, 1975, I was born an overcomer, the fourth living child of my mother and the third of my father. Upon entering the world, I can only imagine my mother looking and smiling at her bundle of beauty, so innocent, pure, and perfect. I often wondered if she knew then I would become an overcomer of the struggles I would face in my early life, would her decisions have been different? I know one thing for sure: She didn't know I would be robbed of my innocence, my purity, and my perfections. From my own motherly intuition, I am sure that had she known, she would have made other decisions.

I believe my maternal grandfather, the late Mr. John Ritchie, must have known I would be a fighter, that giving up would not become a part of me. You may want to know why I came to this conclusion. This is the reason: I asked my mother to explain the rationale behind my pet name, Bet, as it isn't a shortened version of my legal name, Diana. She explained, "When you were born, you were full term, but you were smaller than a premature baby. Everyone thought you wouldn't live, so your aunt and I made a bet that you will live. However, the moment your grandfather saw you, he took you into his arms and looked at you and said, 'This one is so pretty, I don't care what others say. I bet you are going to live a very long time, long enough to become a woman."

And that was how my nickname, Bet, came about. Such a bet on my life! Yes, my grandfather did love me. I remember him telling my grandmother the spoon was too big for me to use. Even though my biological father named me, to this day I prefer to be called Bet.

I never held either of my parents accountable for any of the obstacles in my life. I may have asked myself "Why me?" but truth be told, I wasn't the only one to have had unpleasant experiences. As I became older and started to interact with others, especially through my work as a juvenile probation officer, I learned to use all my negative experiences and turn them into positives. This is my struggle, my defense, and my success. This is the strategy of my life.

Moving Forward

Chapter 1

My Journey, My Life, My Story

My father left my mother and me when I was four months old. Being a single parent of four with no career, my mother needed help. She asked my grandparents to raise her daughters at their house in the county while she stayed in the city and worked. She did what she thought was best at the time. With the care they provided, growing up with my grandparents was a wondrous experience. Life wasn't always cookies and cream, of course, but without a doubt, they did their very best. They couldn't afford luxurious things, but they provided the most important foundation of my life. They taught me morals, work ethic, self-discipline, self-respect, self-resilience, and how to love and respect others. They made sure I went to school and to church—I had to be in Sunday school every week, no excuses, no complaints. Most importantly, they gave me what was missing: mother and father love. They weren't just my grandparents; they became my mother and father.

My mother would visit us in St. Elizabeth when she could. I couldn't wait to see her, knowing I would be getting a new dress, a pair of shoes, or hair bows. Even so, the thought of seeing Mommy made me anxious. Although I was only four years old at the time, I still vividly remember my grandmother receiving a letter from my mother, which my oldest sister read aloud: "I am leaving to go abroad for a while, to seek a better life so I can be more financially stable to take care of my kids." My eyes filled with tears; I wasn't sure if I would ever see her again. I didn't understand at the time, but as I got older, I learned to appreciate the decision she made. She wanted to bring us with her to the United States, of course, but there were legal procedures she had to follow. The first step was filing the necessary paperwork for us to join her in Florida, which she did shortly after arriving. (It was to be a long process, I would soon to find out.)

I also learned to appreciate Clinton, my favorite uncle, the one and only Mr. Clinton Ritchie, as he would often refer to himself. (Rest in peace, Uncle C. I miss you dearly.) Back then, I didn't know who he was; I'm not sure if I had even heard his name. When I became an adult, though, I realized he was the one who gave my mother the opportunity to make a better life for herself and us.

Living with my grandparents, siblings; Michelle, Sandra, Joy, and Meleshia,, Cousin Nazel, and Cousin Gary delivered both good times and bad times. My grandparents made sure I was fed, clothed, and attended school. With the help of financial assistance from their other children, they provided everything I needed. Even when others chastised them about their decision to raise my mother's five small children (stepladders, they called us), they endured and protected us. Of course, my grandparents were older and couldn't do as much physically. Still, they did not spare the rod and spoil me, not at all. They believed in Proverbs 13:24: "He that spareth his rod hateth his son, but he that loveth him chasteneth him betimes."

Unfortunately, they could not protect me from everything. I was sexually abused by two adults, my Uncle Ben (not his real name) and a distant relative, Aaron, from a very, very, tender age until I was twelve. With Uncle Ben, it always began the same: "Come Bet, let's go get water." (There was no running water.) "Come Bet, let's go get firewood." (We used fire for cooking.) And unless I wanted to be hit, I had better not refuse his orders. If I told anyone, he threatened, I would go to the New Market, what we called the town jail. "It's all right," he told me. "Just lay down and open your legs." I remember my tears, him telling me to "Stop the noise; I'll finish soon." After it was over, I was told disdainfully to "Get up and clean yourself," as if I had been the one asking him to do what he did.

At the time, my grandparents had two houses within walking distance of one another. We all lived in one during the day, but at night the kids slept in the other, as my grandparents' home was too small for everyone to fit comfortably. It was at the older house where we slept that I would be called to go for water and firewood. Remembering those times now, I am filled with an anger I thought I had long put away. My distant relative would sneak into the house when I was alone, force himself on me, and then leave. He tried his best to reassure me everything was OK; besides, he told me, even if I said anything, no one would believe me. After the third time, I learned not to stay in the house alone.

My mother visited us for the first time when I was about eight years old; of course, the sexual abuse stopped while she was home. But then, four months before my tenth birthday, it stated all over again, this time lasting until I was twelve. When my uncle Ben was caught doing the same thing to another minor, I could see the hurt and pain in my grandmother's eyes. Nothing was done about it, though; no charges were filed. But my own abuse stopped.

The Bible says, "My people are destroyed for the lack of knowledge" (Hosea 4:6. I understood and learned this concept the hard way. Of course, if I knew then what I know now, the situation would have been different. There would have been the one attempt, of course, but that's as far as it would have gotten. But I lived, and I learned.

Reminiscing on my life, I have had some extremely difficult experiences. I was sexually abused; I was raised without either of my biological parents; I came from a less fortunate background; due to a lack of money, I stopped attending school a few weeks into ninth grade—and yes, I became a single teen mother. But the older I got, I began to realize no one is exempt from unpleasant times. I realize the impact from these experiences could have destroyed me; instead, they made me a stronger person, the person my grandfather saw when he first laid eyes on me at the age of seven months: Bet, the fighter, the overcomer. When I was young, I had no knowledge of the concept of *risk factors*. I didn't know all those experiences were risk factors for juvenile delinquency, criminal activity, or prostitution, or that they often extinguished the motivation to thrive, to strive for a more successful and meaningful life.

Am I completely healed of all the hurt and pain? After years of self-reflection, self-help, and recovery, yes. But the memories are still there—and they're not going anywhere. I was able to forgive both of my relatives and move forward. I am no longer ashamed to share my experiences with others. I'll admit, the abuse negatively impacted some areas of my life, especially in terms of relationships, but I never allowed all the abuse and pain to control me. Even with all that was happening, I did well in basic and all-age schools (from pre-K through middle school) and kept up my participation in church activities. The more I suffered inside, the more I had to find something else to focus on—so I studied. In this way, I admired my grandmother. Even though she did not have the opportunity to attend school, she vowed that all the children she raised would attend at least to the ninth grade. (At the time, free public education in Jamaica ended after ninth grade and my grandparents could not afford the tuition.)

As I got older, life changed; no more abuse was the greatest gift imaginable. I looked forward to when my uncles, aunts, and other family members would visit from abroad. I couldn't wait to receive all the clothes and gifts they would bring. By the time I hit my teenage years, my mother would send money, too, and our quality of life improved. Whereas before I sometimes walked four to five miles each way to school with no shoes, now I had shoes on my feet. No more going to school barefoot!

Being less fortunate will either make or break you. It can motivate you to strive for something better. Alternately, you can let your misfortune dictate your future, accepting the situation and giving up, no longer aiming for a better life. Even as a young adolescent, I vowed to use all those negative situations to motivate me, to become successful. Even then, one of my most important vows was to protect my children if I ever became a mother.

My Biological Father

It was a day I thought would have changed my life for the better. I don't remember the exact date, but it had to be a Monday, Wednesday, or Friday in the summer of 1991, when I was fifteen. I know it was one of those days, because at that time, our post office was only open three days a week. My grandmother received a letter from my mother's sister that read, in part: "Bet's father came to see me and asked about her. I told him where she is, and he asked me to write to you to see if you would allow Bet to meet him."

All this time, he knew where and how to locate me but had decided not to. But it didn't matter then; I was so excited to visit my father. I was filled with the feeling of, "Oh, here's the opportunity I've been waiting for." Maybe it would be a new start for me, and I could reenroll in school or get a job. (Really: Who would hire me at age fifteen?) I remember, three months prior to my sixteenth birthday, riding on a bus all day to see him, from my grandparents' home in St. Elizabeth to his cousin's house in Kingston, and then to my Aunt Merlene's restaurant in Port Maria. When I finally arrived, he was at work, so I stayed at the restaurant until he got off work. I must have waited there for five hours.

As I sat on a stool at the counter, countless men came into the restaurant; oddly, it never crossed my mind to look at them and wonder if any of them were my father. It's rather amazing that, as soon as this man walked in—this man I had never laid eyes on, not really—I knew it was him, and surprisingly he recognized me. He came to my table and said, "What is your name?" and then, before I could answer, he asked, "Do you know who I am?" I never wanted to refer to him as Father, Dad, or Daddy, as he had never been that to me. But on that day, I said, "I guess you are my father." He nodded and said, "Yes. I am." He was very quiet and reserved (traits I now see in my oldest son).

We stayed at the restaurant talking for hours, trying to get to know each other. He asked about school and wasn't pleased when I told him I had dropped out. But who could he have blamed? He had abandoned me for the first fifteen years and nine months of my life. Even with the reality of my life, with all I had been through, I was not angry with him. He apologized for not being there as I grew up. He did not make excuses or try to pass the blame.

I stayed for a few weeks, but it felt that, although he was trying, he wasn't trying hard enough. I didn't stay at his house; instead, I stayed with my Aunt Merlene and her two sons. She was very nice and treated me as her own, even for the short time I was there. One day she saw me combing my eyebrows (I didn't know anything about waxing then; I looked like a werewolf) and said,

"Diana, pretty looks won't help you; you need an education." I didn't learn to appreciate that comment until nearly twenty years later.

My father wanted me to stay and enroll in school, so he took me to St. Mary Technical High School to be tested. Of course, I had already been out of school for almost two years and my academics weren't up the high school's level. The principal called my father and told him, "I can't enroll your daughter. She can read, but not that well." (I still don't understand her definition of "not that well." The way I remember it, I read the entire passage without missing or mispronouncing any of the words.) But because I could not attend school, I went back to my grandparents' house.

Six months later, I again went to see him. This time, the visit lasted for a month and it seemed to go well; however, a few weeks after my return home, I received a letter from him. Anxiously, I ripped open the envelope, thinking (wishfully, it turned out) he had sent me money. Instead, he said I should just stay with my grandmother until I was able to join my mother. I was hurt. Although I did not want to live with him, I really wanted a relationship with him. Then I caught myself, asking, "Why am I so hurt?" He was just another man to disappoint me.

I never wrote him back. What would I have said, that my feelings were hurt? No; then he would have known I cared, and that was something I could not disclose. Back with my grandmother, sixteen going on seventeen, I just wanted a new start; however, each time I went to the United States Embassy, I was denied a visa. Life was normal but getting older with no plans and no opportunities for advancement was not where I wanted to find myself. But as Sam Cooke sang, "It's been a long time, a long time coming but I know a change gonna come, oh yes it will." And oh yes, it did!

Change

After the sexual abused ended, when I was thirteen years old, I had my first secret boyfriend: Steve, the boy next door. He was only two years older than me. We were always caught together, and I took the punishment from my grandmother and older sister accordingly. I grew to love him, but by then he had moved away to the city, visiting only twice a year. He returned when I was sixteen and we resumed our relationship. I got pregnant the first time we had sex (consensual), during what should have been my first pleasant experience.

And so, my change came in May 1993. By then, I was five months pregnant, but I hadn't told a soul. I was scared. I was going to be a teen mother with no plans, no income, nothing. It was time to go back to the United States Embassy to be interviewed for a visa. Although my mother had been filing for me to come to the United States since I was eleven, I had been denied a visa for over five years because of her poor financial status. It turns out that, when petitioning for a family member to be granted permission for residence in the United States, the petitioner (my mother, in my case) must prove herself financially capable to care for the dependent (me) without the assistance of the State (welfare).

But back then, in May 1993, the interviewer turned me down again. "I can't let you go to your mother," she said. "She is ill, can't work, and does not receive enough money to support you." I looked her in the eye and said, "Life can't be any harder with her than what I am living in now." She asked me to explain, so I did. I explained everything. I told her about not attending school, a lack of funds, and an elderly grandmother who couldn't continue to care for me. For the very first time, I broke my silence and told someone, her, about the sexual abuse I had endured. She took pity on me, granting me the visa and telling me I had six weeks to leave Jamaica. Afraid it would have ruined my chance of getting a visa, I did not tell her I was pregnant.

I vividly remember walking out the embassy, overwhelmed and scared: overwhelmed with the joy of finally being able to join my mother, but scared that I was pregnant. I called my mother to give her the good news. She was happy, of course, but could sense my mixed emotions. "What is it?" she asked. "Why don't you sound happy?" I didn't know what to say, so I simply said, "Nothing. Nothing is wrong." I rushed home to tell my grandmother the news. True to form, my God-fearing grandmother said, "Thank you, Jesus!"

Chapter 2

Relocation

And so, began the new chapter in my life. On June 24, 1993, I departed Sangster's International Airport in Montego Bay, Jamaica, for Orlando International Airport in Florida. The thought of leaving Jamaica filled me with mixed emotions. It was terrifying; it was exciting; it was breathtaking. I was accompanied to the airport by my grandmother, sisters, and cousins. The last thing my grandmother said as I boarded the plane was, "Remember what your grandfather and I taught you: Get an education, don't forget where you're coming from, remember your father, and take the name of Jesus with you."

I was ready for the change, "the good life," I thought. I honestly didn't think there would be any hardship. It didn't take me long to figure out there were struggles and challenges everywhere, even in the United States of America. Even then, I was aware that environment, financial status, and family dynamics can influence our future in terms of success; however, I knew the key word was *influence*, not *determine*. We must face all situations head-on, control what we can, and always, always focus on improving ourselves.

When I arrived at the Orlando airport and saw my mother waiting for me, I began to cry and couldn't stop. Unfortunately, they weren't tears of joy. I had no idea my mother was so ill, but there she was wearing neck and back braces and leaning on two crutches. The tears soon turned to admiration, though; even now, I am amazed by her strength and tireless effort.

I didn't tell my mother about my pregnancy, but in August, she found out. Then seven months pregnant, I wondered how I was going to provide for my unborn child. I needed medical care. I needed all the provisions to prepare for having a baby. I had no source of income and my mother was unemployed. I was in America, and the struggles began anew. My mother took me to the Florida Department of Children and Families to apply for Medicaid. How else was she going to pay for the birth of my child? I felt so ashamed; I had barely been here two months and had already added to her burden. Life was an ongoing challenge, I found. I was seventeen years old, seven months pregnant, with little education and no employment. It certainly wasn't the best way to enter adulthood.

School/Birth of My Firstborn/First Job

Summer was over and it was time for the new school year to begin. My mother intended for me to go to school; however, she had no knowledge of the education system here in the United States. She was unaware that, despite my being pregnant, I would still have been able to go to a traditional public high school. (In Jamaica, females weren't allowed to attend public school while pregnant.) However, having completed only the eighth grade four years prior, I scored too low on the Test for Adult Basic Education to be placed in the General Educational Development (GED) program. Instead of retaking the test, I opted for a study review course. After completing the study course, I was enrolled in the General Educational Development program so I could earn a GED certificate. And so, began my daily five-mile roundtrip walk to the center and back, as my stepfather had to work, and my mother was unable to drive. I felt so uncomfortable walking every day while I was seven, then eight, then nine months pregnant. Adding to my discomfort was the fact I was the only teenager in the classroom.

The GED program was challenging. I was in a new country, a new school, and facing motherhood; everything had changed. However, I managed to cope. One day as I was sitting in class, a fellow student, Ureeda Menzies, walked over. She asked, "How old are you?" I told her: seventeen. "When is your baby due?" "October," I said. Next, she asked, "Do you have everything you need for your baby?" Shamefully, I lied and said yes. She then got to the point, asking, "Why are you not in regular high school instead of the GED program? You are so young!"

Before I could explain, she gave me information on the process to get enrolled in the teen parent program through the local school board. The teen parent program was designed for pregnant and teen mothers who were still attending school. A child care center was also on campus, so we were able to take our babies to school. When I walked into class the following day, the teacher said I was needed in the front office. When I returned to the classroom, I was surprised with a very nice baby shower (my first experience of such an event!). I was overwhelmed with gratitude; I had absolutely nothing for the baby until that day. I received a baby carrier filled with baby wipes, diapers, lotion, shampoo, oil, blanket, onesies, and washcloths. There were enough supplies to last for over two months. I couldn't walk home with my arms full, so one of the ladies gave me a ride. I'll never forget the care they showed me

As I headed home one Friday evening, a young lady asked me when I was due. "Sometime this month," I told her, and she replied, "Doesn't look like you have much longer to go." She was right: I had my baby two days later.

I gave birth to my precious little bundle of joy, Tiffanie (named by my younger sister, Eleanor, who was so excited to be around a new baby; when she asked, I couldn't dare say no), on October 10, 1993, and just like that another chapter of my life began. Of course, I received Women, Infants, and Children (WIC) services and Medicaid assistance; for the other needs, I was reliant upon my mother for two months, until I found a job. I couldn't attend class during my six weeks of recovery; however, I did enroll in the teen parent program and was scheduled to start in January. Finally, the first day of school came—and I missed the bus. I was so disappointed (and later learned the bus went to the address next door).

The U.S. educational system was very different from what I was used to. I was so lost in the beginning, but I quickly adapted; I was determined to earn my high school diploma. Because I was eighteen years old, I was enrolled in the performance-based program, which provides an avenue for students who are over the age of eighteen and behind in credits to complete high school before they turn twenty-one. The requirements for this program were to earn fifteen of the twenty-four required credits to successfully complete high school and earn a GED. Although I did well in my classes, I struggled with time management, as I had to be on the school bus at 5:45 a.m. and did not get home until almost 4:00 p.m.

My job was bussing tables at Stacy's Buffet. Although the chain has since closed, it was long known as "the worst buffet in the area." I remember the day I walked into the restaurant enquiring about employment as though it was yesterday. I asked the supervisor if he was hiring and he told me no. I looked him directly in the eye and said, "I need a job today." When he asked if I had any work experience, I was honest, telling him, "No, but I will give it my best." He smiled and told me to come back at four, dressed and ready to work. I was so excited. My daughter was eight weeks old, and I would finally be able to take care of her financially.

Although my work schedule was from 4:00 p.m. to close, I was late for work every day. Luckily, my supervisor understood, as he knew I didn't get home from school until 3:50 p.m. Although my work shift ended at 10:00 p.m., my lack of transportation meant I often wouldn't get home until 11:30 or 12:00. Before I had a job, classmates sometimes made fun of my daughter's clothes because I couldn't afford much; now, she looked as cute on the outside as I knew she was on the inside. (Times sure have changed, though, as one of these classmates had to ask me for assistance a few years ago.) I was doing well, working and going to school, and finally, after a year of saving money, I was able to purchase my own car—a 1983 used red Cutlass Supreme—and move into a two-bedroom duplex with my sister, paying my own rent. I was making progress, moving on up like the Jeffersons; sometimes, though, the "moving on up" feeling doesn't last long.

One day, the school guidance counselor called me to her office. She told me I had earned all my credits but failed the GED test and would not be able to graduate. I was shattered. I had failed. I could no longer attend school. I was so mad at myself; I had broken my mother's heart again. Since I had moved out, I had made it a practice to stop by my mother's house on the way home from school. This time, when I arrived, she asked me why was I there so early. Ashamed, I told her I had been sent home; I did not successfully complete the GED and I wasn't able to continue attending school. Although she didn't say much, her face told me how disappointed she was.

But I was determined; I didn't give up. I enrolled in the GED program at South Florida Community College (now South Florida State College in Avon Park). I had my choice of three weekday sessions: 8:00 a.m. to 11:30 a.m., 12:00 p.m. to 3:00 p.m., or 6:00 p.m. to 9:00 p.m. I was so eager to retake the test, I dedicated myself to attending two sessions daily. After six months, I thought I was ready to retake the test—and I passed. I felt like I was on cloud nine when my diploma came in the mail. I was overjoyed; I had achieved something big! Finally, I made my mother proud as the first of her children to earn a high school diploma.

But that one piece of paper wasn't enough; I knew I could do more. But how was I going to further my education without money? I couldn't afford to pay for classes on what I made at the restaurant. I knew what I had to do: work two jobs and save for college. Unfortunately, the idiom "one step forward, two steps backward" had my name written all over it, as my dream of holding down two jobs to save for college was soon shattered. At the end of my shift one night, the supervisor called a staff meeting to let us know this had been the last night Stacy's Buffet was open. I felt as though my world was caving in. I had bills—rent, utilities, car payment, auto insurance, and caring for my daughter—now with very little money to cover them. I struggled greatly but, with the help of unemployment pay, I managed. A few months later, I found a new job as a convenience store cashier and College Savings Plan 101 was back on.

Resources

As it turned out, I was working in the right place at the right time. The convenience store ended up being the place I learned about enrolling at South Florida Community College and the financial aid assistance that was available. Although I had earned my GED through the college, I didn't know a thing about enrolling in regular classes. One day at work, I was introduced to the new hire, an older lady named Caroline Smith (who remains my best friend to this day). She wasn't altogether pleasant to me at first, although she later explained she had had her share of poor experiences with Jamaicans. One day, she warmed up and asked me, "What are you doing here during school hours? Why are you not in school and who are you related to?" I told her I had completed high school and was working to save money for college. She surprised me, asking, "Why are you saving money for college?" I thought her question was bizarre; how would I attend college without paying for tuition?

Her explanation opened a world before my eyes. "You don't need money for college," she said. "You can apply for financial aid and that will pay for your classes." Despite providing me this helpful information, her prejudice came back as she said, "That's what wrong with you all: Come here from another county, don't ask questions, yet want to get ahead. How?" I tried not to take offense, as I really did appreciate her input. She instructed me to take off work the following day and go to the school's financial aid office. I did as I was told—and that was the start of my college educational journey.

I remember it like it was yesterday, walking into the financial aid office and telling them what I needed. I didn't know how to fill out the financial aid application. "For the sake of time," said Ms. Sandy, the financial aid clerk, "I will complete it electronically for you." I was overwhelmed with gratitude. In Jamaica, there was no such thing as financial aid. How could I have known it was different in the United States? It didn't help, either, that I was also too timid to ask questions. Ever since I had arrived in Florida, I had endured so much teasing because of my "Jamaican accent." I was always told *"Go learn to talk"; "Learn to speak English"; "Go back across the water"*; and *"You all come over here trying to figure things out, trying to take our jobs."* Because of these attitudes, I soon became self-cautious and reserved.

Chapter 3

The Beginning of My Education

As my college journey began, I began to worry. Maybe I wasn't as smart as I thought I was. Maybe there was no way I could do this. Because I hadn't done well on the college entrance test, I first had to take a handful of preparatory courses. It was hard and frustrating, and at times, I really wanted to quit. But I owed it to myself and my daughter to earn an education and improve our quality of living. I also felt I owed it to my father to follow through on his instructions—the only thing I ever got from him except for my given name. In the short period of time I spent with my father, he gave me one valuable piece of advice: "Try to earn the highest level of education there is or seek a career; this will give you a sense of independence. When you become a woman and a mother, you will be able to take care of yourself and your children if the father decides not to take care of his responsibilities. You will never have to depend on any man if you earn your own money."

My experience with the Associate of Science program was like I had never attended school before. Even though I started by taking three classes, two were prep courses so I was only earning three credits per semester—but I was determined. Working two jobs, raising my daughter, and going to school was challenging. Between the convenience store and a job I had recently gotten at Wendy's, I worked from 5:00 a.m. to 1:00 p.m. and from 4:00 p.m. to 1:00 a.m.), with my three classes scheduled in between. The owner of the convenience store gave me permission to clock out early when I had class; I would also take off Wendy's on the days I had night classes from 6:00 p.m. to 9:50 p.m. Of course, both work and school schedules took a bit of juggling with each new semester; thankfully, I had two supervisors who understood my priorities. I managed not only to attend class and hold down two jobs, but to buy my first starter house, a place to call home for me and my daughter.

During the third year of working on my general business associate's degree, I realized I needed to start thinking about a career. I applied to be a youth care worker at Avon Park Youth Academy, a juvenile offender residential commitment facility. When I got the job earning three dollars more per hour than Wendy's or the convenience store, I decided to quit my other jobs so I could concentrate more on school. Now, with just one job, I was able to take four classes instead of three, moving toward graduation even quicker. Thankfully, my supervisor, Marvin, would change my shift each semester to accommodate my school schedule, something I more than appreciated.

As I am writing and reminiscing, I can say this new challenge was well worth it, as I had to complete one level to get to the next. Sometimes we aim too high, wanting to reach the top without first starting from the bottom and working our way up. We must understand that, 99.99% of the time, this won't work, instead creating additional obstacles to overcome.

Failure/Discouragement

One of the biggest discouragements during my educational journey came from the one who should be my greatest encourager. Two years into the program, at the age of twenty-three, I gave birth to my second child, a son I named Tevaris. Unfortunately, he wasn't healthy as baby, suffering from a range of health issues. When he was five months old—immediately after the semester add-drop date—he was hospitalized for a week and a half with asthma and RSV. At the time I was taking four classes and working at the juvenile facility. My days consumed with having to stay in the hospital with him or waiting on an infrequent volunteer to sit with him so I could attend class, I had no extra time to ask my professors questions concerning the lectures. I was the last student to arrive and the first to depart. At the end of that semester, I failed three of my four classes and earned a C in the fourth. I cringed when I saw my grade report and my newly lowered 2.0 GPA.

Unfortunately, I experienced the same obstacles the next semester. Again, immediately after the add-drop deadline, my son was admitted to the hospital, and my days staying there with him resumed. I remember getting to English class one afternoon so tired I slept through the entire lecture. At the end of the class, I went to the professor's desk to ask him for the handouts. Before I could speak, he said, "Diana, what is going on with you? You arrive late, you're the first to leave, and you slept during the entire lecture. You did this last semester, too," he added. In tears, I apologized and then explained my situation. He looked at me with genuine sympathy and said, "Don't stop coming and do the best you can." That semester, I again failed three of my four classes, earning a single C in that English class. I honestly believe the professor gave me a passing grade just for showing up; there's certainly no way I could have earned it. Because of this, I always tell my children I am not sending them to school to earn a C for their presence.

At that point, my GPA fell below the 2.00 minimum eligibility for financial aid assistance. Now I could only attend if I paid for classes out of pocket. How could this have happened? I was earning $8.00 an hour. I was taking care of my two children and now had a mortgage. Classes were $50 per credit hour, for a total of $150. But what choice did I have? So, I sacrificed and made the decision to take one class per semester; that was all I could afford. I scheduled an appointment with my guidance counselor, walking into her office with confidence because I had figured out a way to continue my studies.

"Based on my grades," I began, "I am no longer eligible for financial aid. I would love to retake one of the classes I previously failed. Do you know if any of them are being offered over the next two semesters?" Turning to her computer, she retrieved my academic history, reviewed it as I waited, and then turned to me with her glasses on the tip of her nose. "Can't you see that you are not college material? You need to find something else to do—get a job in the convenience store or something—because college is not for you."

At that point, I could have allowed her to shatter my educational journey. I could have responded angrily, chastising her for trying to push me back where I came from. But right then, sitting in that chair, I decided to take all criticism constructively. I knew she had her education and I was trying to earn mine. I took a deep breath to calm myself and asked the question again. I told myself that when she said I can't, I will show her I can. She doubted me, and I was determined to prove her wrong. She saw failure; I saw progress. It's OK to fail, I told myself, but not to give up. She took a moment to consider my request, and then said, "I will enroll you in Liberal Arts Math, but you will need to pass it with an A." The class was only offered at the satellite campus, which meant I would have to drive thirty minutes to and from class. But I didn't mind commuting; I had to chase my dream.

I earned an A in that class, and then did the same in the next class the following semester. Life has a way of taking us on different journeys down different paths, and these paths are not always smoothly paved; in fact, some of them are downright rocky and at first glance seem impassable. At times, we may never understand the journey or the paths, but we have to take control of our destinies. There's always a purpose in life, and it's up to each one of us to identify ours.

Challenges/Transition/Success

After successfully completing both classes, I was taken off academic probation and became once again eligible for financial aid. The days began to blur as I continued to work, attend school, and care for my children. Many times, it appeared to be a never-ending process, but I looked at it like an investment: The more I invest, the harder it is to let go. Most importantly, I told myself quitting wasn't an option, not ever. So, although I struggled, I remained focused. As it turned out, a degree that should have taken me two years to complete dragged on a full six years. Despite my determination, I couldn't help but be a little angry at myself. "Six years!" I exclaimed. "I could have earned my Master's degree!"

Finally, the time came: I completed my associate degree. I was told I would receive my diploma in the mail, but I waited months and it never arrived. And so, in the oppressive July heat, I loaded the kids in the car and drove to the college. Walking toward the registrar's office, I was met by a friendly-looking woman who greeted me warmly. "Are you a student?" she asked. With pride, I told her I had recently earned my degree. She smiled, congratulating me. "Do you want to continue your education?" she asked. I sighed. "I would love to," I said, "but I am unable to leave home and live on a college campus because of my children." She introduced herself as Mrs. McKenna, a representative from Webber International University, and said she could enroll me in the Bachelor of Science program today. Webber International University, I learned, was located thirty-five minutes from my home, which meant I could commute.

She needed my college transcript from South Florida Community College to get me enrolled. Together, we went to the student services department to obtain my transcript—where the clerk told me I did not complete my associate degree. I almost fainted; I assured her that I had. Upon reviewing my academic history, she exclaimed, "Oh, I see. You did successfully complete all required courses; however, you did not pay the graduation fee of twenty-five dollars." I felt so silly. Of course, I had been aware of the graduation fee; however, I thought it was required only if I participated in the graduation ceremony, which I had not done. I clearly remembered consoling myself about missing the ceremony, but it was true: I didn't have the funds for that, as I had my children to care for. My heart dropped; I didn't have the twenty-five dollars. When Mrs. McKenna saw my face, she said to me, "Don't worry; I'll pay it for you."

Finally, the fees were paid, my diploma was issued, financial aid was procured, and I enrolled in Webber International University to start my bachelor's program. Because I had already spent an extra four years on my associate degree, I wanted to complete this program in two years. I was determined to do just that, signing up for five classes each semester. Yes, it was an overload—but I was an overcomer! I attended class six days a week while still working my full-time job. I was physically, emotionally, and financially drained; there were days I couldn't afford gas to get to and from school. I quickly learned about the gas on credit, getting a charge account from a privately-owned gas station, and then paying it off weekly or biweekly. The downside of this was that gas was always more expensive, but at least I could get to class. I did my best to remain consistent, persistent, dedicated, and focused. I knew the hard work would eventually pay off—and I wanted it.

Still, I struggled. Some days, it sounded as if the lectures were in French and I, of course, only knew English. How could this be? Simple: I either didn't understand the subject or hadn't had enough time to study as thoroughly as I should. I pushed myself to do my best on written assignments, which I mostly scored well on. However, as I was still uncomfortable with public speaking, I avoided all my oral presentations, guaranteeing myself zeroes on those assignment.

One day, I had an essay due at 8:00 a.m. on a Saturday morning, I got off work Friday night at 1:30 a.m. and did my best to write the essay. I knew then it wasn't at all what was expected, just the best that I could do with a pressing deadline and a lack of sleep. In a very small font, I wrote in the footer, "Please excuse all the grammatical errors and the lack of knowledge on the topic. Blame it all on the late-night hour." Even with that lackluster assignment, I ended up earning an A in the class.

But, I did it. I successfully completed within the two years, earning my Bachelor of Science in Business Management with a minor in Finance. Once again, I didn't want to participate in the graduation ceremony, as I couldn't afford a new pair of black shoes and the only ones I owned had scraped-up heels. But my mother and Caroline felt otherwise. They insisted I participate, as I hadn't "walked" with the previous degree. Besides, they reasoned, it would be a great event for my children and younger sibling to see. So, I told myself I would walk across that stage for my family—my mother, stepfather, and younger siblings—my friend Caroline and most importantly, my two babies.

In July 2004, in my scraped-up heel shoes, with my head held high, I walked proudly across that stage in the presence of my family, Caroline and another friend of mine, Ilett. As I crossed to shake the dean's hand, my son, who was almost five years old, yelled out, "That's Bet!" That was one of the proudest moments of my life. My mother was full of pride, both for me and for herself, as I was her first child to graduate from college. It didn't matter there were three Ds on my transcript. I had a piece of paper in my hand that meant far, far more.

Four months after completing my bachelor's degree, I was hired as a juvenile probation officer, the first full-time role hadn't even applied for. A former coworker joked with me, saying, "Bet, you finally got your first real job." Giddy with excitement, I simply smiled and said, "Yes, sir." Everything was progressing. Finally, I had a normal schedule—Monday through Friday, 8:00 a.m. to 5:00 p.m.—and I was off every weekend. I was able to spend quality time with my children, attended their school activities, and even take them to Jamaica to meet the rest of the family and see where their mother grew up.

Even with all these riches I'd never had before, I still dreamt bigger. I was considering enrolling in the online University of Phoenix MBA program, but I wanted to learn my new job before taking on another challenge. And then, in the spring of 2005, my life changed when I met a gentleman, a minister. One day, my coworker stuck her head into my office to tell me "a guy" was in the lobby to see me. A guy? "What guy?" I asked her.

She replied, "Not sure, but apparently, he doesn't know your name, as he asked to see the Black lady."

"So how do you know he is asking for me?" I said. "I'm not the only one here."

She smiled. "He said it wasn't me or the supervisor."

Once I arrived in the lobby, I recognized him as someone I had seen on campus but had never spoken to. He smiled, introduced himself as Levon and then explained the reason for his visit: He wanted me to go out with him. After having not dated for almost five years, I decided to give it a try. He was good looking, soft spoken, and handsome, so why not? He also represented a "safe" dip back into the dating pool. As he was a minister, there were specific rules about dating he had to follow. I was also very active in my own church, having developed a personal relationship with God, so our dates mostly consisted of attending church and going out to eat. When we weren't together, we spent hours on the phone, even taking every chance we could get to call each other while at work. True, he was handsome and smooth, but what drew me to him the most was the fact he was a Christian. It didn't matter that he had no money;

what mattered was the way we connected on a mental and physical

level. He was also the first man to ever show genuine interest in me.

A year into our courtship, he called and suggested we go to

the mall. It wasn't usually a place we spent time, but I agreed. Once

there, he said, "Let's look at jewelry."

"Why?" I asked. "I don't wear jewelry." He just laughed and

steered me to the store. We looked at necklaces, bracelets…and

rings. One of the rings caught my eye. "I like this one," I said,

smiling.

One evening, I got home to find him on my porch, the ring in

his hand. First, he prayed over it, and then he asked me to marry

him. Although a twinge of concern hit me regarding his financial

status, I figured we could work, earn, and make a life together. I

smiled and nodded, telling him yes.

Two months later, we bought a home together, and in June

2006, we were married. Finally, my son had a positive male role

model in his life. Levon was a wonderful, caring, attentive dad to

Tevaris. He invested a lot of time with my son, introducing him to

sports and other father-son things. We prayed together, worshipped together, and went through life together as a family. Even though we were struggling financially, it was a good life.

Within three months of being married, I was expecting my third child. (Never again will I doubt a woman who says the protection failed.) With another baby on the way, we figured another source of income would be beneficial, so we started a cleaning business. I gave birth to my second son, Tavious, in May 2007, seven weeks early. He was a fighter at birth, just like his mother. (I often look at him and remind myself how grateful I am to have him. I would be one lonely soul if he wasn't around.) While on maternity leave, I finally decided to enroll in the online MBA program. I figured it would be much easier now, as I had more physical assistance around the house. Ironically, getting my Master's degree proved to be a much smoother path than my previous college experiences. I remember sitting at my desk, baby across my legs, while I tried to get my assignments completed.

As with everything, though, there are pros and cons. There I was, trying to be a mother, a minister's wife, and a full-time student, working full time and going to church three times a week.

Sometimes there just weren't enough hours in the day to conquer all the tasks in front of me.

I recall one night in particular, I had an assignment due by midnight, it was 10:30 p.m., and all I had completed was the title page. True to form, though, I continued to balance life's responsibilities and completed the MBA program within a year and a half—with a 3.76 GPA. I decided that, even though I was low on funds and the graduation ceremony was four hours away, I wanted to participate. On December 6, 2008, I proudly walked across the stage in the presence of my husband, our children, one of my brothers, and, of course, Caroline. Despite all the people in the auditorium cheering for me, I couldn't help but feel a bit hurt, as my mother felt the drive was too much and decided not to attend.

Life continued to progress as it does, everything seemingly normal until one day everything changes—especially with my marriage. It felt as though I had taken a nap and woken up in a different world with a different husband. Cheating, lying, dishonesty, arguments, disrespect—you name it, he gave it to me. I remember telling myself I would not retaliate, and I didn't. Instead, I continued to focus on my children and how to shield them from all that was happening. After marriage counseling didn't work and his abuse started to become physical, I realized the only answer was separation. Even though I didn't yet file for divorce, I had been done with my marriage since the day I started putting all my personal items in my purse, worried about them being taken. When he called me by his girlfriend's name, I felt hurt at first, then disgusted.

Through all that had been going on, my heart never allowed me to render evil for evil. I remember one day, while driving him to his doctor's appointment, we were having a pleasant conversation, during which, he called me by her name. All I said was, "I hope you heard yourself." There was no apology or empathy on his part. I just laughed and said, "Life."

After we separated, I received a call one day with his apology. He told me, "I really want to come back home, but I am ashamed. You are a wonderful woman. After all I have done to you, you still haven't changed one bit. You are better than me; I am not good enough for you."

My heart softened. I replied, "We all made mistakes. You are forgiven; I will never hate you. But yes, the marriage is over." By then, he had lost his job and broken up with his girlfriend, so I let him move back in and stay in the guest room until he found another job. As he suffered from a range of medical issues, I also accompanied him to doctors' appointments when needed. I had been hurt so many times in my thirty-three years that I had become almost immune to the cycle. Instead of fighting, I learned to let go and walk away, even when it's eating me apart on the inside.

I was once again a single mother, but now to three children. As a result, the financial struggles were more intense. I went to the bank to check the balance of the little money I had, only to find it had mysteriously disappeared. My account balance was in the negative hundreds of dollars in overdraft checks fees. To make matters worse, Levon hadn't paid the mortgage for months, despite telling me otherwise, and the house had gone into foreclosure. I didn't know what to do. I had no one to assist me financially. I couldn't borrow from my friends or family even if I wanted to; as it turned out, I owed them hundreds to thousands of dollars I hadn't even known about. My only option was to withdraw the money from my oldest children's college funds. I managed to take the house out of foreclosure, paid all the overdraft fees, and repurchased the furniture that had been repossessed. Of course, there still wasn't enough money, and before long, the house went into foreclosure again. Luckily, I was approved for a home modification loan, saving my and my children's home.

I didn't think things could get worse, but they did; the struggle was harder than before. With no reliable transportation, a child in daycare, and a son in private school (public schools had been unable to meet Tevaris's needs), and all the other responsibilities, I accepted a part-time job with a cleaning service on top of my full-time job as a probation officer. Now, after working days Monday through Friday, I cleaned banks after hours and on Saturdays. Every day at 5:00 p.m., I would drop my son off to sports practice, and then drive around town to clean banks while my daughter was home with her little brother. Before long, all four of us were cleaning the banks together. Even though I was working sixty hours a week, I was thankful to have a part-time job with somewhat flexible hours. A strict schedule would have put too great a responsibility on my daughter, who was in high school at the time. Also, stricter hours would have meant my oldest son would no longer be able to participate in sports activities, which he loved.

I remember being so financially unstable, my mortgage was always a month or two behind. The reality was, whenever I paid my mortgage, I was unable to purchase anything or pay most of the other bills. I couldn't have been more grateful when Caroline brought groceries and clothes and school supplies for my one of sons. Even going through these hardships, though, I decided not to apply for welfare, worry incessantly about child support, or ask my children's fathers for anything. If they offered, I would accept, but it wasn't my job to demand they take care of their responsibilities. They were adults and should have acted like it.

Prior to the separation, I had applied to the Ph.D. program at Walden University and was waiting for a reply. Upon acceptance, I once again applied for financial aid and decided to start the program. I figured being enrolled in school would give me something else to think about besides all the problems going on. I knew the major challenge would be time management, especially with me already working two jobs. I asked myself, "Bet, do you really want to take on this challenge now? Will you be able to be focused and dedicated? Will you have the time to invest in studying?" I literally answered "no" to each question. Then I remembered the one instruction I had received from my father. I also reminded myself that time waits for no one; if I waited until I had the time, then I would never do it.

After starting the Ph.D. program in September 2009, I attempted various schedules but with no success. As soon I settled down and logged on my computer after work, I would fall asleep. I tried getting up early in the morning to work on my assignments, but that didn't last, either, as I would be physically awake but mentally asleep. I decided to dedicate all day Saturday and Sunday evening to working on my assignments; however, that turned out not to be feasible, either. My oldest son would usually have a game first thing Saturday morning, which meant we would spend just about the entire day at the game. I also realized that working on assignments only on weekends was not going to work.

To remain on track with learning, understanding, and completing the assignments, the school recommended a weekly investment of twenty to twenty-five hours per week. I finally committed to investing at least three hours every night. After leaving work at 5:00 p.m., between my son's sports and my second job, I would get home about 9:00 p.m. Then, after ensuring my children had completed their homework, eaten, and gotten into bed, it would be 10:30 p.m. before I sat down at my computer. I would work on my assignments until 2:00 a.m., then 4:00 a.m., then 5:00 a.m., only to be up for work by 6:00 a.m. I would also spend my lunch hour conducting research. I was determined.

My divorce was final, and I had started to mingle with another friend, Andrea, who told me to stop hiding and come back to church. I had been staying away from all my church friends, as I was too ashamed of some of the things that had occurred during my marriage. But I couldn't return, not yet. I wasn't ready to face everyone. I was ashamed: of what had happened during my marriage, of how short it had lasted. Although a weight was off my shoulders, I was still in financial shambles, still trying to provide the same quality of life for my children, and still pushing myself in school.

Part of attending an online university for your doctoral degree was the face-to-face interaction of residencies, four of them. The time had come for my first residency: five days in Virginia. I was concerned but filled with gratitude when my sixteen-year-old daughter reassured me, "Don't worry; I will take care of us." I said to her, "So you are going to get up at 6:00 a.m., make sure everyone is dressed, take everyone to school, and assume the role of a parent for five days?" She nodded and said, "Yes." And she did, wonderfully. I was able to attend the residency without worry; of course, I returned home to see that all went well. (Thanks, Tiffanie; you really did an awesome job.)

My second residency was in Jacksonville, Florida, two hundred miles from where I lived. I still didn't have a reliable car or the money to rent one, or even to purchase meals. But I had to attend. I emailed my residency group and asked if anyone from the Tampa area was attending, thinking we could carpool and both save some funds. Thankfully, one of my fellow students did respond. I explained my situation and humbly asked could I ride with her, and she said yes without hesitation. I offered her forty dollars to assist with gas; it was all I could do. I packed some snacks and TV dinners and decided that would have to work. Rather than staying at the residency hotel, I made a reservation at Extended Stay USA, as it was within minutes of the residency and considerably less expensive. Although I had no money when I made the reservation, I knew I would get paid on Friday, two days before the Sunday checkout. I thought payment would be due upon checkout, but I was wrong.

Unfortunately, as I was checking in, I was asked for payment. I told

her I thought I could pay upon check out. Desperate, I asked her if

she could hold the room for me and she said she would. As I was

walking away from the counter, a lady sitting in the lobby looked at

me and asked, "Are you here for Walden?" When I said yes, she

gave me a warm smile and said, "Me too." Her name was Judith; we

are still friends to this day.

I walked outside to call the one person I knew would help

me: Caroline. She chastised me for traveling so far without money,

but she agreed to help. Within the hour, she called back with the

transfer confirmation number. And here came another issue: Western

Union was on the other side of town and I had no car.

I truly believe there is always a guardian angel, someone in

the right place when needed. Returning to the front desk, I told that

the clerk I had the money; however, I had no transportation to get to

the other side of town to collect it. She immediately softened. "Don't

worry, she said." My shift is about to end. Give me a few minutes

and I will take you." And she did. I offered some money for

gasoline, but she smiled and said, "My good deed." Later that night,

I learned the woman who had given me a ride to Jacksonville had the same issue with prepayment, so although I had only reserved a room with a single bed, I invited her to share. (Since that time, whenever making reservations, I always ask for two beds, never knowing if someone might need help.)

Thankfully, my third residency was also in the state of Florida, this time in Miami. Although it was only three hours away, I still had no transportation; I had to leave my car with my daughter so she could drive herself and her brothers to and from school. As before, I also had no money to rent one. Discussing residency accommodation with Judith, now a close friend, I told her my first hurdle was to figure out a way to get there. Although Judith lived in Georgia, she generously offered to drive to Sebring and take me to the residency. "Are you sure?" I asked. "Have you considered the distance?" I could hear the smile in Judith's voice as said, "Just be ready when I get there." I will forever appreciate my friend, whose generosity allowed me to successfully achieve yet another milestone.

Through the struggles, challenges, and hardship, I continued to motivate myself to complete my educational journey. I was determined never to allow the "lack of" to deter me. I also wanted to provide a good example for my children.

In 2011, I reconnected with Gray, the first guy I had dated after relocating to the United States. After my failed and painful marriage, I was scared, but I decided that since I already knew him, I could relax and reestablish a relationship. At first, like most relationships, everything was great. I loved spending time with him—and truth be told, one of the greatest benefits was having someone to explain the assignments I was struggling with. After eleven months, he asked me to marry him. I had been down that road already and it didn't work, so I said no. But after seeing his tears and what seemed to be sincere love for me, I relented and told him yes.

My fears were realized when, after we got married, he changed. Every negative experience I had encountered with Levon resurfaced: cheating, lying, humiliation, physical abuse, and disrespect. This time, though, it was a thousand times worse than before. Again, I was trying desperately to protect my children. I tried to pretend all was well, although, of course, they could see right through the pretense. The relationship became so toxic, I often had to call the police, once three times in one month. I became so distracted that it was almost impossible to focus on school, but I buckled down. I didn't quit; I drew upon my self-resilience and kept pushing myself. I had been through hardships before and was determined to achieve my goal no matter what. In less than a year, our marriage had ended, but Gray refused to leave my home. It was painful and angering, but what could I do? It set me up for the biggest regret in of my life: having my children exposed to such toxicity.

I endured the frustration and turmoil of cohabitation, for two almost years, until I finally gathered the strength to put it to an end. I packed all his personal belongings and took them to his mother's house. I was met at the door by one of his sons, who said, "I'm glad you finally woke up. What took you so long?" Instead of taking justification from his words, I instead felt less than a person. Two years later, I filed for divorce.

I was more broken than I have ever been as an adult. I knew I had had difficulties balancing my time between husband, children, school, and work. Levon had been unhappy with the way I always put my children first, even at the expense of sexual interest in my husband. Even with all his apologies and repetition of "It's not you, it's me," I was in a constant fight with myself not to think I wasn't good enough. I felt my self-esteem going out the door; I was so close to allowing myself to become a victim of circumstances and give up on my dreams.

As I learned during that dark time, feelings of worthlessness can cause us to second-guess our own potential. Nonetheless, I trusted God; I knew who I was in him and realized that He must have a plan for my life. I practiced daily self-affirmations, telling myself I was more than what men saw in me. I took a break from school to refocus, as I had submitted my proposal to my dissertation committee four times, and four times it had been denied.

My proposal was rejected five times over three years: twelve quarters of blood, sweat, tears, and tuition money. I was beyond frustrated; the extreme self-doubt returned. And then I remembered what one of my professors had told us during my first residency, that earning a doctoral degree is not an easy or simple task. He also shared with us that his own proposal was denied twelve times before it was approved. If he was a successful college professor and had gone through more than double the rejections I had, I could certainly do it, too. I used his shared experience as a motivation to continue.

Knowing I was struggling and wanting to keep me motivated, Andrea would constantly ask, "When will you graduate?" If I expressed frustration or self-pity, she went into the role of cheerleader. "You can do it," she urged. "You just need to push yourself."

My chair had previously recommended I change my qualitative research design, which necessitated rewriting much of the proposal to realign the revised problem statement with the study. I was crushed; it was almost like starting over. Still, I had disregarded her suggestions for so long, and where had it gotten me? I had no choice but to follow her advice. After I submitted my proposal the sixth time, she approved it. Finally: Success! Next, it went to my committee member for his approval, which came quickly. But I wasn't there yet. The next step in proposal approval is the University Research Reviewer, or URR. Whereas I had chosen to work with my chair and committee member, the URR is a member of your dissertation committee who is assigned by your university. I was upset when I received a denial; she felt the proposal read more like a phenomenology approach instead of a case study. Then I looked at her feedback and realized she was right. After I made the corrections and resubmitted my work, it was approved. I had overcome the first major hurdle!

Next up was the data collection phase, which soon proved to be another big challenge. Although I knew the population I wanted to study, it was hard to secure participants. But I did it. Within a year, I managed to recruit my sample and conduct the interviews. I wrote chapters four and five of my dissertation—the research results and the conclusion—and submitted my manuscript for approval. It was approved without delay. Finally, I was scheduled to complete my dissertation defense.

One week prior to my oral defense, I was sitting in the doctor's office with one of my sons. He had ongoing medical issues and a few surgeries, but I have always dealt with the issue calmly; I knew we would always get through it. But this time was different. I thought my world had ended when the doctor called me into his office and said that my son had multiple sclerosis. I went home and called my chair, telling her what I had learned and that I needed to reschedule my oral defense, I explained why. She was very understanding but did not agree to a postponement. "We will do this together," she assured me. "You have invested years in the process and you know your research inside and out. You are strong, Diana; you will do fine." And so. I prayed and persevered.

I wasn't sure I would be prepared, but I did my best. At the end of my oral defense, after I had presented my dissertation and answered my committee's questions, I heard the words that changed my life forever: "Dr. Clarke, you have done well." On August 13, 2017, a month shy of eight years spent working on my doctoral degree—Public Policy and Administration with a concentration in Criminal Justice—was conferred. Five months later, on January 20, 2018, I attended and participated in the graduation hooding ceremony. I was proud of myself, yes, but the most rewarding part was to watch my children enjoying the moment. Their mother had done it.

Chapter 4

Prior to applying to Walden University, I worked in the juvenile justice field for eleven years, six at the commitment facility and five in probation. Observing the recidivism rate, the offenses, as well as the age of the juveniles, I wanted to gain a better understanding of what was causing these juveniles to commit such serious offenses at such a tender age. I strongly believe if the root of the issues is identified, then appropriate treatment can be administered, with the goal to reduce and or deter future offending. My questioning led to my applying to the Ph.D. program. Although my intent has been to earn a degree in criminal justice, I found it was only offered as a concentration, not a major, so I opted for public policy administration.

Approaching the dissertation process, I decided to conduct my research on juvenile recidivism. Since this is such a wide area, I narrowed the focus to risk factors for juvenile delinquency and juvenile recidivism. Because there are numerous risk factors, I centered my study on six of them: parent criminality, mental health disorder, substance abuse, school experiences, peer pressure, and age of first offense.

Risk Factors for Juvenile Delinquency and Criminal Activities

Risk factors are conditions associated with a higher likelihood of delinquent acts, such as engaging in problem behavior, dropping out of school, and encountering trouble with the law. Risk factors include variables such as family makeup, poor education, substance abuse, sexual abuse, coming from an impoverished or low-income family, and mental health disorders that predict a high probability of later offending.[12] The more risk factors present, the higher the risk for juvenile delinquency and criminal involvement.[13]

Most of us have experienced one or more risk factors, but we have to make a decision. Do we allow them to cripple us, or do we use strategic planning, resources, and self-resilience to assist us in moving forward with our lives? How can we move forward from all the hurt and pain, the fear and doubt, the humiliation, the

---

[1] Clarke, 2018
[2] Farrington et al., 2012
[3] Carr & Vandier, 2001

worthlessness we feel inside? I learned the hard way. It's difficult, especially when we're fighting with ourselves.

On the other hand, overcoming adversity can be easier than we think once we become aware of who we are in God and His plans for our lives. With this knowledge, we can conduct our own individual self-analysis, improve in areas as needed, and eliminate all that is hindering us from moving forward. Although it had taken me years of struggle, I knew I had to get to that place, and I did. As Proverbs 3:5-6 states, "Trust in the Lord with all thine heart and lean not unto your own understanding. In all thy ways acknowledge Him and He shall direct your path." Believe me, this instruction works.

As you can see, I had more risk factors than most. I endured sexual abuse; I struggled with poor academic achievement; I lacked a parental bond for most of my childhood and adolescence; I had an absent father; I was a teen parent; I came from an extremely less fortunate financial background; and was the victim of physical abuse as an adult. I wouldn't say I had mental health issues, as I had never been diagnosed with anything; however, the sexual abuse caused mental anguish, leading to significant symptoms of clinical anxiety and depression. I suffered silently for years. Even at this point in my life, when I've achieved my dreams and overcome massive amounts of adversity, I still endure the negative effects. There are times when I relive the encounters as they happened, remembering the fear, hurt, threats, feelings of being dirty, crying from the pain—and most of all, not being able to tell anyone.

Sexual Abuse/Physical Abuse

Childhood sexual abuse may be related to substance use or involvement in the juvenile justice or criminal justice systems and the experience of post-traumatic stress disorder. The pain of PTSD, of constantly reliving the horrific experience, strengthens the relationship between sexual abuse and substance use, mostly for self-medication.

A large body of cross-sectional research provides evidence of abuse being correlated with delinquency. Rates of childhood abuse are disproportionately high among adolescents involved in the juvenile and criminal justice systems. Sexual abuse victims are more prone to promiscuity and have a high risk of involvement in prostitution. Writing this, I acknowledge that the fact that all the good deeds I have done were not enough to save me; it's only by the grace of God I am not included in these statistics.

But I did not escape the repercussions. I didn't like men for many years. Due to my past trauma, as at times I had felt no affection, no compassion, no feelings or sexual interest. Over the course of my life, I have had one long-term boyfriend, two marriages (lasting a combined two and a half years), and on-and-off friendships lasting no more than three months, and all of them failed. Shortly after we were married, I remember expressing to Levon my lack of sexual interest, although I was too ashamed to explain why. He acted understanding at first, but later used it against me as a defense for his selfish behaviors.

This leads me to Genesis 50: 20: "As for you, you meant evil against me, but God meant it for good." I strongly believe there are circumstances you and I will never understand and can never change yet are unable to avoid. Yet do I allow them to conquer me? Do I subject myself to what overwhelming research tells me? No! Rather, I always strived to beat the odds and achieve a better me. And I succeeded.

Poor Academic Achievement

Studies have linked educational aspirations and underachievement to negative behaviors, which can lead to juvenile delinquency and criminal acts. Low academic achievement can often lead to acting out and result in disciplinary actions, such as out-of-school suspension and/or expulsion. Academic failure is associated with being suspended or expelled from school, which is a major reason adolescents drop out. Academic failure is identified as a risk factor with a high possibility of contributing to juvenile delinquency and criminal involvement. It should be also stated that high school dropouts account for eighty-two percent of the adult inmate population. You may be a middle school or high school dropout, your reading abilities maybe below average, and you may believe there's no hope, there's no way you can start over at this point of your life. I was once at that point. The truth is, it's never too late. Remember, nothing beats a trial but a failure. So, start your journey today!

Poor academic achievement also suggests substantially lower income and a marked increase in the likelihood of criminal involvement and incarceration. You may want to pursue an education but don't know how and where to begin. Take it from me: There is always hope and there is always time. The time is now. I remember vividly how in August 1993, having completed only eighth grade four years prior, I took the Test for Adult Basic Education in hopes of joining the GED program. With my scores below average, I couldn't even receive placement into the Pre-GED class; rather, I was placed in a class to study, and then retake the TABE test.

As I write my story, I feel the sense of accomplishment and joy, remembering my educational journey. I urge you to step out of your comfort zone, put your doubts and fears behind you, and don't be embarrassed; just make that start. I can assure you that once you have completed your journey, you will experience a sense of accomplishment that only you will be able to describe. One of my classmates in the GED class was eighty-two years old, at the beginning of her education. I share this to let you know, no matter your age, you are never too old to start. Don't focus on the time it will take you to complete your degree or vocational trade certificate just focus on completing. The race is not for the swift, but for those who endure to the end.

Lack of Parental Bond

One of the most important connections a child can experience is that of secure attachment through a parent-child bond. It strengthens relationships; it molds us into the men and women we ought to become; it provides a positive adult role model. Albert Bandura's social learning theory best explains this concept. Parents are the first teachers in their children's lives. Human behavior is learned by observing and modeling the behaviors, attitudes, and emotional reactions of others.

Although my bonding experience was less than ideal, I have never blamed my mother for leaving us behind. She did what she thought was best. Rather than abandonment or neglect, it was a survival strategy. However, had she not made that decision, I would not have these experiences to share with you as a motivational tool, and I likely would not have accomplished all that I have. I learned and accepted that the road to success is never smooth. It's a tough lesson to be sure, but in my case, it was a necessary one—and a chance to overcome.

The lack of positive parent-child bonding has been as a predictor for negative behaviors, criminal involvement, and, in my own terms, generational curse. Hirschi's social bond theory explains that children's parental attachment deters antisocial behavior, because the children are able to imagine their parents' reactions to misconduct when temptation arises. Time invested in children is associated with the child's well-being. When the parent-child bond is weakened or broken, offending behaviors begin. Strong connections between children and parents discourage negative behaviors during adolescence.

But what can be done if, for reasons beyond our control, we are unable to form a bond with our parents? Do we use this excuse as permission to give up and become victims of our circumstances? Of course not. We exercise self-control; we seek strategies to move beyond our lack and work to achieve. Perhaps, like me, you were never taught this lesson, in which case you're likely asking how this can be accomplished. For me, it was a tremendous challenge—and there are still challenges—but I made the decision to do more with my life, not become what society or researchers predict.

You might be a single parent or one of two parents in the home, yet, regardless of your efforts, you still find it difficult to financially support your children. But don't leave them behind! Although your intentions might be good, as my mother's, your leaving could lead the worst to occur. We never know what will happen until it does—and when it does, it can bring a mountain of pain, hurt, anger, hatred, unforgiveness, and lifelong brokenness. I realize not everyone will agree with me, but I've had a lifetime of lessons. I believe parents and those with whom we entrust our children are and should be the greatest protectors for our children. I recognize there are instances where parents abuse their children; I also know that, in most instances, more harm is done while parents are absent.

Absent Father

The strongest support of the family dynamics should be the father. It was ordained by God that the man should be head of the household. The paternal figure should be the provider, protector, and teacher. He should be the one who treasures his little girls and models for them the positive characteristics they someday want in a husband. A dad should want to be there to guide his kids into adulthood. I didn't feel the full effects of my father's absence until many years after he left my mother and me. Once I hit my teenage years and then the older I got, the more I wished he was an active part of my life. Even now, there are times I look at my children and wish they had known him, that he had been here to spend time with them. But the saying is true: There really is no use crying over spilled milk. I can't dwell on the past and use the excuse "because my father wasn't there." I refuse to.

I am not blaming all fathers who are or were absent. Sometimes dads are absent because they are forced to: court system, custody battles, and ineffective co-parenting all play a role in separating dads from kids. To all fathers who fought for their rightful places in their children's lives but were denied, I appreciate you. Though you may have lost the battle and much or all of the quality time with your children, I consider you awesome dads and winners because you didn't give up. My own father wasn't absent because he was forced to; he wasn't denied visitation or couldn't afford to see me. He simply decided to not be involved. Funny, because I still loved him.

What does research say about children with absent fathers? Some say growing up without a dad can negatively shape us into who we are or who we become. But is this completely true? I'm not in a place to either credit or discredit this statement. What I will say is there comes a time when the decision, the direction, is ours. We must take control of our lives and own what we become. My pastor once asked this question of the congregation: "Can one become successful without the guidance of the parents?" The answer is yes; choose your own path and follow it. Will it be easy? Of course not. But is it attainable? With the guidance of God, absolutely.

Having an absent father can cause self-esteem issues, which may diminish children's confidence in their own abilities and their value as a human being. It can also limit their ability to achieve success academically, professionally, socially, romantically, and personally. Struggling to maintain positive relationships is another negative side effect. I have struggled and do struggle with this, even now. It took me years to notice I had built a wall around myself. I closed myself off from males, from romantic relationships, and I always left before they did. After the pain my father had caused, I never wanted to let myself be hurt by another man. And yet I did. Despite my intentions to protect myself, I still had more than my share of disappointment, hurt, confusion, abuse, and failed relationships.

My greatest rejection from a man, always, will be that of my father. Not the day he left me as an infant; the day I received his letter in 1992, telling me not to come back and visit. I had been so hurt, I ripped up the letter and tossed it into a pit toilet. My intent was to bury the memories of him in the toilet, but my heart wouldn't allow me to. I didn't respond until a few years later, when I sent him a Father's Day card. My grandmother had taught me to never treat others the way they treated me, but to treat them better, and that's what I did. He called then to thank me, letting himself cry while professing he wasn't expecting anything from me.

Researchers have shown having an absent father can also cause depression and lead to early sexual promiscuity. I can't honestly say I experienced depression, not really, and of course, I sheltered myself from men. The fact is, a healthy father-daughter relationship is vital, but the lack of it doesn't stop a woman from becoming who she aspires to be if she wants it badly enough. For me personally, that meant becoming a positive, God-fearing, powerful, influential, and successful woman, mother, and wife to a loving and respectful husband…one day.

Teen/Single Parent

Was it a generational curse or what? My mother was a single parent, my sisters were single parents, and then I, too, became a single parent. Married to my grandfather all her life, my grandmother was the only one who had done it differently. I wondered what had changed from her to my mother, my sisters, and me? Why didn't we follow her example and emulate her as a role model?

As a single mother, I learned to become both the mother and the father, as I had to assume the responsibilities of two roles. I'm not alone in this, as I know countless other single parents have had to do the same thing. Needing to shoulder all the responsibilities on my own shaped me into someone different. Because I was a single, teenaged parent with no education, employment, or plans, my future back then didn't appear promising. But I drew upon my past, the pain I'd endured and all that I had lacked, to set goals, define my values, and hold myself up to a standard I'd created. I needed to build a better foundation for my children than I had received. The generational curse stopped with me; I never wanted history to repeat itself in my household.

One of the most important decisions I made was to continue my education. Yes, it was the most challenging thing I had ever done, and sometimes I'm amazed that I made it. But with strategic plans, resources, and resilience, along with my stubborn determination and trust in God, it was doable. And remember: Would anything truly worth it be easy? Of course not. We must want it hard enough to work for it.

Teenaged single parents and their children are at a high risk for poverty, depression, and drug and alcohol use, and often become long-term recipients of welfare. Here are some of the staggering statistics[4]:

---

[4] Teen Pregnancy Prevention, National Conference of State Legislatures

- Mothers below the age of nineteen years are sixty-five percent more likely to experience poverty compared to mothers over nineteen.

- Thirty percent of teenage girls who drop out of high school do so because of pregnancy or single motherhood.

- Fifty-two percent of mothers on welfare had their first child in their teens.

It's up to us to prevent ourselves from being just another statistic. We must get to that point to say, "No, not me. No more excuses!" One thing I realized is that there is always *better*. But better certainly wasn't coming to me; I had to be proactive and determined to achieve it.

Maybe, like me, you were unable to complete high school, to earn your diploma. Maybe you, too, walked to school because your single mother didn't own an automobile and you couldn't afford a bus pass. Maybe you're pregnant right now and you have no idea how you're going to afford to feed and care of a child when you can barely do the same for yourself. Maybe you've been evicted from your apartment for not paying rent, forcing you back into the home

of an abuser.

Let me be the one to tell you, right here and now: Don't give

up.

Chapter 5

The Process

Based on research and statistics, I should not have achieved a future of success. (I am aware we all have a different perspective, a unique definition of success, so insert whatever yours is here.) But those factors were only predictions, not predeterminations. The only thing that is predestined, the only thing we can't change, is death. There is absolutely no escaping death—for me, you, anyone. But I dug deep and utilized my capacity to achieve my goals.

But achieving doesn't mean I am done. I am still working on becoming who I aspire to be. I am still working on my career, wanting to research and implement prevention and intervention tools to reduce recidivism among juveniles. I am working on becoming a clinical director at a female residential facility. I am working to achieve my goal of owning and operating my own therapeutic group home for female victims of abuse. I am still working on getting closer to God. I am still trying to maintain a positive outlook on life.

I am still working on being more influential and motivating others, which is why I decided to write this book.

Thankfully, life is a process that doesn't stop until God takes us home, and I will never arrive at the point in life where I stop trying to improve myself. Sure, there have been detours. There have been obstacles. There have been failures. I have experienced many, many moments of wanting to give up. But I stayed focused. One concept I exercised during my journey is that of *rejuvenation*. When the circumstances became overwhelming, I rejuvenated myself and started where I left off. I needed to exercise resilience, too, as there were many times I had to quickly recover from difficulties and failures.

From being a sexual and physical abuse victim at a tender age, a middle school dropout, a teenaged single parent, and someone who grew up without any parental bonds, I became a successful woman with a doctoral degree—rather commendable, I think. I'm telling my story to let you know that you, too, can move beyond all your hardships, overcome your risk factors, and attain a better life. Don't bury them, as I had done for years. Feelings don't stay buried for long; they always find their way back to the surface. Don't use your participation in church, work, or school as a means of forgetting where you came from. I did this for far too long, from a very young age. But it all came back to haunt me during those quiet times when I become less preoccupied and my own thoughts crept back in. Finally, I realized my means of coping weren't working—so I changed my strategies.

Finally, at the age of forty I did what I should have done a long time ago: I asked God to take away my plagues. I called them out by name. I asked Him to give me the forgiving heart. If I had forgiven so many others for their wrongs, why was I still carrying all the pain of my abuse and the absence of my father? So, I gave the pain to God and forgave my trespassers.

I am no longer ashamed about the situations that shaped me. No more excuses, no more being in bondage. I also accepted the fact that none of what happened to me can be undone. The facts of my past will never change. The day my guidance counselor's words crushed my heart will never go away. All the damage were already said and done. Now it was up to me to figure out how to get past it all. So not only did I ask God to guide me, but I *allowed* Him to do so. I know I can do nothing on my own, but through God who is within me. "To God be the glory, great things He hath done. All honor is given to Him." Even with all my determination, focus, and hunger to overcome, I could not have done it without asking God to guide my path.

Earning my doctoral degree was not an easy task. At the time I enrolled in the program, I was at one of the lowest points of my life: emotionally, financially, personally, and spiritually. I was motivated to enroll in the program for various reasons, perhaps the biggest one being to set an example for my children that, regardless of circumstances, the sky truly is the limit. I also wanted to encourage my siblings to start their own educational journeys, and to fulfill the one instruction my father ever gave me.

One of my goals in life, always, is to have a positive impact on others. One of the greatest challenges in my educational journey was time. Between working two and three jobs, being a single parent to three children, staying active in church, assisting others, and trying to keep my sanity, I was always wrestling with time constraints. But as I learned, if we wait on time, we would still be waiting.

Inspiration

My profession allows me to work closely with young ladies. Through interacting with them, observing their behaviors, and learning about them, I realized most of them have experienced, and are often still experiencing, some of the same risk factors I had. Therefore, my passion is to reach out to them, to provide guidance in any way I can.

As I was sitting in my office one day, reminiscing about my life and brainstorming how to better serve my clients, I asked myself some questions: What can I do to reach them? How can I help start them in a different direction, to convince them they are more than just a court order? I needed to tell them there is so much more to life than what they currently knew, that change is within them. I thought it would help them to know that I was once in their situation, but I rose above it. I didn't allow myself to remain stuck in self-pity and distress.

With all that I've learned, with all that I've been through, and with my position now, it would be selfish not to work to help others. Life should never just be about S-E-L-F. Luke 32:22: "But I have prayed for you, that your faith fails not: and when you have returned, strengthen your brethren."

While I was in my office questioning myself, God gave me the answer. He was very clear. "Write a book, a motivational book," He said. "Tell your story through public speaking." I laughed so hard that Jeneen, my coworker, playfully dialed our crisis center and told them to come to get me; she thought I had lost my mind for talking and laughing to myself. I shared this vision with a few people, but still I was hesitant. I refrained from writing the book, as I was very concerned about the impact on my family. Many of these stories had never been discussed and, truly, some things are best left unsaid. I will always do everything in my power to not hurt anyone's feelings.

Though I didn't start writing a book, I moved forward with telling my story through public speaking. I also founded a nonprofit organization, Move Beyond, Inc., with the vision of influencing young adults to use their strategic planning, resources, and self-resilience to move beyond past failures and doubts and toward success. The organization's mission is to strengthen our communities by empowering young people with knowledge and guidance to reach their full potential through mentorship, education, and positive relationships. (A huge thanks to all the board members—Shayna, Shemina, Andrea C., Jeneen, Andrea F., and Orenthol—who have worked hand-in-hand with me to execute this mission and vision.)

One of the main events of Move Beyond, Inc., is our annual Motivational Summit. We seek out individuals from all walks of life who have not allowed life's setbacks to prevent them from achieving their dreams, encouraging them to share their experiences and the strategic tools they used to move forward.

Ultimately, though, I had no choice but to write this book. I have one friend, Beryl, who would not stop urging to follow my vision. There were times we'd be listening to others who would touch on issues of my own. When this happened, she would look at me and say, "Hurry up and write your book before others think you are stealing from them." And so here I am.

The goal is not to seek sympathy, but to let others who have experienced or are experiencing similar issues know they can overcome, they can succeed. God didn't create the problem without the solution. Now that you know what the problems are, focus on the solution. It is within you through the grace of God.

Your Change Is Within

Now that I have shared some of my life, my journey, and my story, now I urge you to take a moment and reflect on your life. Ask yourself, "Have I experienced any of these or other risk factors? How can I move beyond them and seek for a better me? Am I satisfied with my accomplishments?" If your answer for any of these questions is no, ask yourself, "What are my goals? Are they clear? What are the plagues that are hindering me from working toward my goals?" And, most importantly, "What do I need to overcome?"

If you are unable to answer these questions in a way that satisfies you, now is the time to become proactive and start your journey. First and foremost, trust God; know who you are in Him and His plans for your life. With this awareness, you can conduct your own individual self-analysis, improve in areas as needed, and eliminate anything hindering you from moving forward in all aspects of your life. Second, forgive. Third, set your goals, seek knowledge on how to achieve them, and follow the instructions you receive from God. Fourth, don't create limitations. Fifth, don't give up!

It's OK to fail, but never to quit. You must remind yourself, sometimes daily, that you can do it. Don't believe those who say you're not smart enough; don't limit your abilities. When you are told you can't, you must prove otherwise. I recommend that you use strategic planning, implementing control mechanisms to guide your journey. There are resources everywhere; you just need to seek them out, ask questions. You will never achieve your goals without using resources, the tools you need to get where you're going.

Self-resilience means adapting through adversity, tragedy, threats, or significant sources of stress. You have the capacity to recover, to strive and to thrive. Use it.

The Mirror Effect

One tool I used over the years in the Man in the Mirror. I am not sure how I came up with this, but it has worked. Years ago, I was meeting with Kiana (not her real name), a fourteen-year-old client who was surrounded by all the risk factors you can think of, including a toxic relationship with her mother. As I was talking to her, I asked, "What are your future plans?"

"I have none," she said with resignation. "I am nothing but a drug user. I have been abused; no one loves me. What plans could I have?"

I was lost for words. I realized that she had been through so much, she had given up on life at such a tender age. I took her by her hand and led her to the bathroom, saying to her, "Look in the mirror and tell me what you see." She started to describe herself as before, and I stopped her. "You are not your situation," I stressed, "and you will not allow it to determine your future."

I also told her to repeat after me. "I am Kiana. I see love, positivity, greatness, and change in the mirror." Emotionless, she parroted my words; I continued, "I am beautiful; I am a person and not a thing. I am smart, and I can become whatever I want to be. I will be successful." I told her to open her mouth and say it like she meant it. "Convince yourself," I urged. It worked! Four years later, I saw Kiana again, and she had made positive changes. She had overcome.

But that day, as I was encouraging her with the mirror effect, I was also encouraging myself. Since then, I have placed a mirror in my office directly in front of my desk; each time I look up, I am looking at myself. It might be a bit vain, but that's not important. My use of mirrors is more mental than physical. Whenever I look in the mirror, I am looking at my past, present, and future. I am reasoning with myself how to keep moving forward. I remember explaining to my daughter the rationale for having mirrors all over the house. She smiled, looked at me, and said, "All this time, I was wondering if you were crazy."

I know there will be times when your past will creep up on you, and you will be slapped across the face with all the hurt, pain, doubt, and self-disgust. You have to stare it directly into the face and repeat who you are at that moment and who you aspire to be. Even with all I've been through, this has worked for me, and I am sure it will work for you. Give it a try! We may never forget the past—and really, why should we? It's what made us who we are today—but we shouldn't dwell on it or allow it to cripple us. Instead, use your past as the tool to push you forward. Regardless of your present circumstances, other people's opinions do not have to become your reality. Identify the greatness within you. Make your parents, your children, and yourself proud. Use your experiences to become the person you want to be.

I became the woman, mother, and advocate I am today because of what I went through. You can achieve such heights of success by turning your struggles and failures into growth and opportunity. You, like me, can overcome.